MY DAD IS A BRO

My Dad Is a
BRO

The Editors of *BroBible.com*

G

GALLERY BOOKS

New York   London   Toronto   Sydney

Gallery Books
A Division of Simon & Schuster, Inc.
1230 Avenue of the Americas
New York, NY 10020

First Gallery Books trade paperback edition May 2011

GALLERY BOOKS and colophon are registered trademarks of Simon & Schuster, Inc.

For information about special discounts for bulk purchases, please contact Simon & Schuster Special Sales at 1-866-506-1949 or business@simonandschuster.com.

The Simon & Schuster Speakers Bureau can bring authors to your live event. For more information or to book an event contact the Simon & Schuster Speakers Bureau at 1-866-248-3049 or visit our website at www.simonspeakers.com.

Designed by Jaime Putorti
Background images from istockphoto.com

Manufactured in the United States of America

10   9   8   7   6   5   4   3   2   1

Library of Congress Cataloging-in-Publication Data

My dad is a bro / The editors of BroBible.com.—1st Gallery Books trade paperback ed.
p.   cm.
1. Fathers—Humor. 2. Men—Humor. I. BroBible.com (Electronic resource)
PN6231.F37M9 2011
818'.602—dc22   2011001899
ISBN 978-1-4516-2773-2
ISBN 978-1-4516-2776-3 (ebook)

Authors' Note

The captions in this book are intended exclusively as humorous commentary based on our reactions to each individual photo—all done in lighthearted fun. We swear. None of the captions should be mistaken for factual or even intelligent statements. We assure you they are nothing more than creations from our own sick imaginations and meant completely in jest to honor all the Bro-Dads out there. Basically, don't take anything we say seriously. We all have deep-seated psychological issues and digestive problems. Just like Dad.

INTRODUCTION

*C*hildren give their fathers many names over the course of their lives. It starts with "Da-Da," which typically comes one to three months after the child's first actual words: "Ma-Ma." (Dad will never let Junior live this down.) "Da-Da" graduates to "Daddy" when baby boy is still crapping his pants, and eventually "Dad" when he is pissing the bed only every other week. That leads to the more emphatic, high-pitched "DAAAAAAAAAAAAAAAAAD!!!" when he almost electrocutes himself or when Mom crushes his dreams of playing tackle football in his bedroom. On the playing field, Dad might be "Coach" or "Pleaseshutupandgobacktothestandsyouareembarrassingme." Lost in a dreamlike state, wandering the aisles of Home Depot, Dad's suddenly "Paging Bob Johnson: your family's looking for you. They want you to come home." When yet another "senior moment" occurs, he's alternately "Pops" or "Old Man" or "Gramps." Then there are the less-affectionate monikers, typically employed post-curfew or midgrounding ("A-hole," "Sumbitch"), as well as the eternally desperate and grateful ("Mealticket" or "Bail").

But for some fathers, the ultimate name isn't bestowed until the kids have left the house, headed off to college, and killed most of the brain cells Dad worked so hard to nurture. It comes on Parents'

Weekend, when Dad is half a case deep and is so dominating on the beer pong table that his son or daughter has gone from focused teammate to admiring fan. When Dad sinks the last cup, throws his hands up in the air, and yells "Who's next?", it suddenly hits home—*Oh my God, my dad is . . . a Bro?*

MY DAD IS A BRO

***S**o what exactly is a Bro?* At BroBible, we define Bros as guys who, no matter their age, are stalwarts of sport, connoisseurs of female beauty, and masters of both channel surfing and sandwich making. Oh, and it doesn't hurt if a Bro knows how to party his face off, too.

So how do you know if your dad is a Bro, especially if he's long since retired from the beer pong circuit? Well, you have to analyze the whole package, from how he raised you, to his hobbies, to even his candor—these are what define him and make him the Bro you came to know and love.

If it wasn't during a beer pong game, can you remember the first time you looked at your father and said, "Yep, now *that* is a Bro"? Was it the time in the ninth grade when he gave a to-the-point birds-and-the-bees speech, simply but elegantly stating, "You'd better not get her, or anyone else, pregnant—you got me?" Or was it the recent spring morning when a mellower version of that same man reveled in his newfound reign over you on the golf course: "Son, what you're doing today isn't considered golf. Look at that divot you just took. It's like you're raping Mother Earth." A father's candidness only adds to his Bro prowess.

Don't worry if you can't pinpoint one eureka "my

dad is a Bro" moment. Being a Bro is a lifestyle, something you just are and don't think about or aspire to be. It happened to us just like it happened to our dads. That is what makes us proud to be their sons and daughters. Proud he is a Bro.

WHAT IT TAKES TO BE A DAD

Being a dad isn't always a pleasure cruise. Sure, you have a handsome kid to look at and say, "God, he's gorgeous—he looks just like me." But other than that, it's a full-time job. It doesn't come with a clock to punch out or retirement to look forward to. Hell, it barely offers bathroom breaks.

Despite the grueling hours, gray hairs, and the inevitable midlife crisis, the truly great fathers forge on. They put down their beers, hang up their clubs or cleats, and become completely infatuated with their children's lives. They would gladly miss a round of golf just to watch their son suck at T-ball. And they'd do it with patience in their hearts and smiles on their faces. It's almost unfathomable, but it's part of the job.

Then, as their children grow up and the headaches become less frequent and severe, dear old Dad is allowed to walk the fine line of father and friend. He can join the party. And he does it like things were done back in his day, when he didn't own a minivan. Dad has always been a Bro—he's just now finally getting the chance to reveal that fact to his kids.

If nothing else, this book is a tribute to those moments, those regressive instances when what it truly takes to be a father is realized. Sacrifice. Loads of it. Instead of reveling in his fading youth, he put it on the shelf to have you. He never forgot it was up there, but when his late nights went from throwing back bottles of Jack to serving bottles of warm breast milk, you can bet the damn farm that he couldn't wait until his kids were old enough for them to meet their real dad: the Bro.

This collection of photos shows all the tomfoolery dads put on the back burner just so they could change diapers, relearn algebra, and receive crappy ties. It's good to see that they can pick up right where they left off.

HOW TO SPOT
A BRO-DAD

Bro-Dads are most easily spotted by observing the following habitats and activities.

⫸ *Golfing*

Dad is a busy guy. Opportunities for him to escape both the office and Mom's never-ending honey-do list are few and far between. A round of golf, however, is one of Dad's favorite excuses to get out of the house, hang with his buddies, and drink all the booze the beer-cart girl can legally provide.

⫸ *Smoking Cigars*

Dad is always coming up with reasons to celebrate with a stogie: a job promotion, a big catch, his team winning the championship, the elementary school graduation of his business partner's nephew. Hell, he's probably stashed a vintage Cuban somewhere in the garage for even the most unrealistic occasion: the day Mom lets him watch an entire football game in peace.

⫸ *Fishing and Hunting*

To Dad, "the one that got away" wasn't some girl he met at summer camp, but rather a 140-pound tarpon he couldn't quite get in the boat. According to his fish stories, that beauty broke both his heart and his

50-pound test line. There's nothing Dad loves more than pursuing the ultimate trophy to hang in the man cave and bragging about his inner-Hemingway.

⫸ *Charming the Ladies*

Your old man is a smooth and charming guy. He doesn't really have to spit game to pick up chicks; after all, he already landed your mom. But in the event he needs to keep his options open, let's just say it wouldn't be too hard for him.

⫸ *Back in the Day*

Before you popped out and began hemorrhaging his hard-earned life savings, Dad was throwing down with the best of them. His hair was Framptonesque and his penchant for raising hell rivaled that of Keith Richards in a brand-new hotel room.

ⅢⅢ➤ *Party Animal*

Although he claims he locked his "Frank-the-Tank" side in a fraternity house basement twenty-five years ago, Dad can still treat a party like it's his business. He applies his old-fashioned managerial style to everything, from meticulously icing down the beer to crafting the perfect late-'70s Yacht Rock playlist. When the party really gets going, Dad jumps on the express train to Passed Out Town, making station stops at Keg Stand Alley and Beer Bong Boulevard before bowing out with an offering to the porcelain gods.

MY DAD IS A BRO

"We're gonna throw a rager,
boy—it'll be just the two of us."

**The last time Dad held his tongue
was when he lost this bet.**

With the right hat, they just
bring you tequila.

"What part of 'Don't take my picture' did you not understand?"

"I'm secure in my masculinity."

To hear him tell it, you'd think
he'd landed Jaws.

"Which one of you candy-asses is up next?"

"Honey, phone child services!
Our boy is about to get a
beating!"

Sadly, this picture with pro
Natalie Gulbis is Dad's greatest
accomplishment on a golf course.

It took him ten seconds to chug
it and then ten minutes to stand
back up.

He may be an ace at Flip Cup,
but his tie collection is a damn
tragedy.

"When I was your age, I could do this one-handed . . . and without slipping a disc."

Dad's tailgating starts in the parking lot and ends with him screaming "don't tase me, Bro" on the 50-yard line.

Nothing says "outlaw biker" like loafers, cuffed designer jeans, and a gold Rolex.

The big kahuna of the backyard
says, "Mahalo!"

"Moondoggie, tell me you remembered to invite the chicks."

With age comes a stocked liquor cabinet.

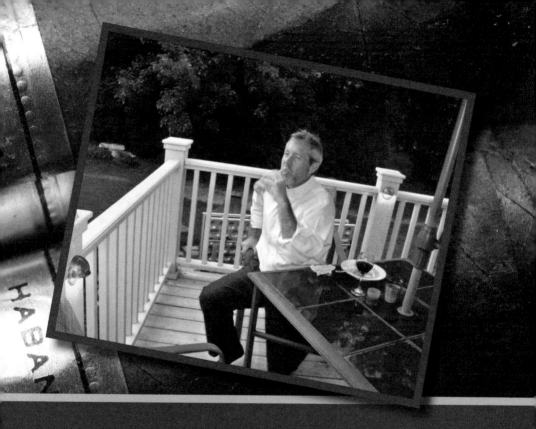

Bros icing Merlots.

Like a fine wine, beer guts get
better with age.

Somewhere, a rival goalie feels a sharp pain in his side.

**Tucker, Cooper, and Skip:
Everyone in this picture is
named after a dog.**

They call themselves "The Busboys" because they clean tables.

With age comes wisdom: Only a
fool would try to run the table
on an empty stomach.

Dad likes his malt liquor like he
likes his women: in the backseat
of a car.

"Quit bitchin' about the top bunk; that's where you were conceived."

Tuesday afternoon's finest.

Rocky Mountain Bro.

You're never too old to learn
something stupid.

"Adjust my hat? I have a guy for that."

Dad likes wings but *loves*
breasts and thighs.

Fisher-Price makes a beer bong?

"I also love straw hats, double bacon cheeseburgers, and hugs."

"Sure, son. We can pretend like
this blue tarp is water if I can
pretend that you were adopted."

Dad isn't forty, he's twenty-one with nineteen years of experience.

"I took a bigger leak in that ocean than BP."

"Keep your head straight,
boy. You don't want to look
ridiculous."

"Dad found his golf ball . . . And
we've found yet another reason why
drinking a beer per hole is a bad idea."

"Screw it, my golf game is already an embarrassment."

"If he can wear overalls, I can
double-fist."

"Super Nintendo, Sega Genesis. When I was dead broke, man, I couldn't picture this . . ."

"Where my harem at?"

The lengths men go to keep their mustaches dry.

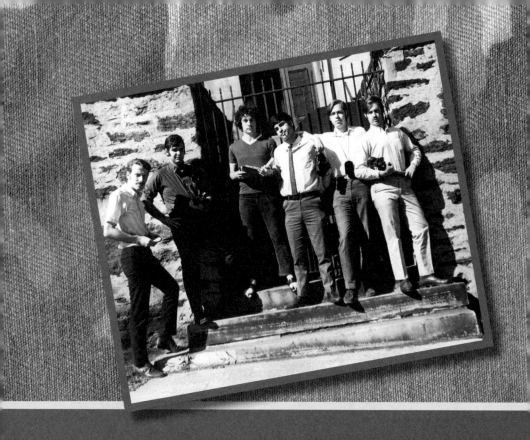

**Dad ran with a gang of toughs
called the Shutterbugs.**

"These are secret teachings—
don't tell your mother."

There's not enough liquor in the world.

Dad supports boobs more than most bras.

"Reeled in your mom the same way."

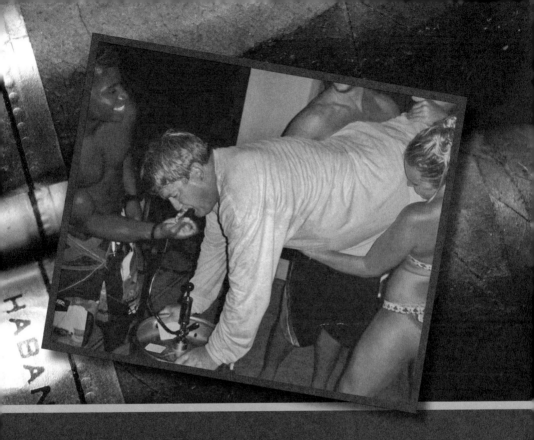

It takes a village.

With each chord, another pair of panties hits the floor.

"The more I drink, the more
likely this car-wreck of a shirt
will come off."

"It's called game, son, and you
have it or you don't."

"Why must we be like that, why
must we chase the cat?"

"King of the world!"

What are his hands hiding?

"You can borrow the plane, son, but not to join the mile-high club."

"No matter what style choices
you make, you're still my boy."

"Here's how you get your money's worth on a booze cruise."

"Bernie Madoff put me back on the pole."

"I rarely use cups . . . bad for the environment."

Not every woman can handle Dad's Flavor of Love.

"But not in that order and never at the same time."

No shoes. No shirt. All service.

"Dad, this is my graduation, not
a popcorn symposium."

How much does Dad love cheesesteaks? Well, let's just say that straw is not for show.

"No, *you're* awesome!"

"It's not technically double-fisting if one's a pitcher."

Just a typical Sunday with Dad . . . outside the Olive Garden.

"This can of beer is to me what
a can of spinach is to Popeye,
minus all coherence and logic."

"This ain't my first rodeo."

"Who are you, TMZ? Stop taking pictures and get in the damn car."

Even vegans eat it.

Loser has to mow the lawn.

Party on wheels.

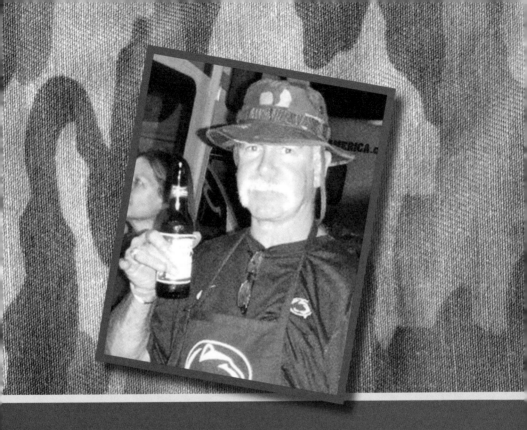

"A gentleman does
his pinky like so."

"Disregard females, acquire currency."

"Get back, vampire, my blood is
pure alcohol!"

Serious business.

"Tramp stamps, twelve o'clock!"

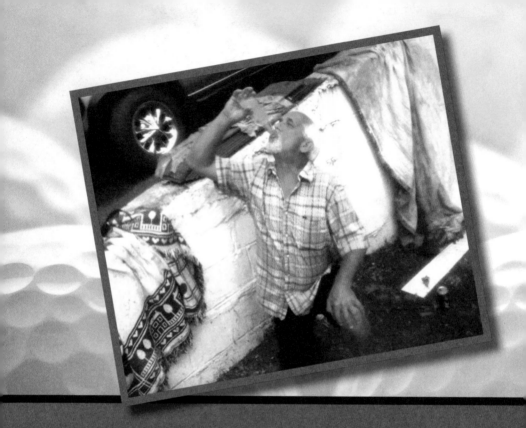

Next time, he'll order his drink neat instead of "on ice."

**Never mess with a man
in critter pants.**

"Henry Hooch is on the case!"

"We got the shot, Dad, now go
put on your costume."

Apparently there's a new fiber supplement called "Buckwild."

Just another Fraturday night.

"'Want to get high?' he asked.
'Sure,' I said."

"You kids can spend all my money,
but over my dead body will you
leave this table a winner."

"I don't care *how much* water there is, don't be so literal."

Weren't those supposed to *stay* in Vegas?

"One down, twenty-five hundred to go."

"I'm drinking a banana daiquiri, but I peeled *this one* just for you."

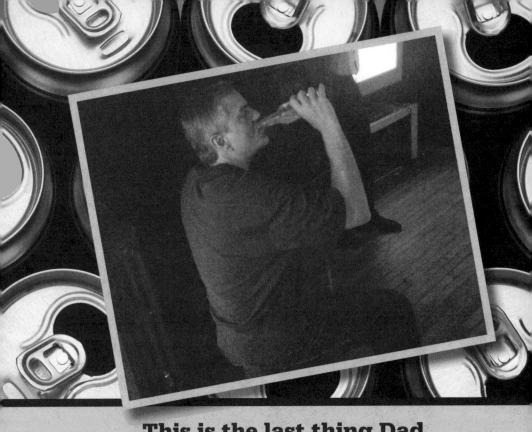

This is the last thing Dad expected when he agreed to "a trip to Iceland."

Mom wouldn't have used a sheet pan, but still a good effort.

In 1979, this look made you a
desired man. Today, it makes
you look like a sex offender.

Family ski trip.

I haven't seen this many shotguns since *The Road Warrior.*

"You'll never get me Lucky
Brats!"

"Can you speed things up, Bill?
This arm isn't bionic."

No glove, no love.

"I always feel like . . .
somebody's watching me."

It's not the genie that makes the wish!

CNBC's Mark Haines enjoys a smoke as he ponders how horrific the world would be if women were in charge of sports.

"Which one of you smells like ass?"

"This glass slipper fits me
perfectly!"

"First you steal my outfit, now you want in on my photo? I don't think so, Marty."

"What has two thumbs and likes it dirty?"

"But . . . my name's Mike?"

Brings new meaning to "Yes, dear."

"Mr. Badass, party of one?"

We wouldn't even ask if that paint was lead-based before we started eating it.

Breakfast of champions.

"Check out *this* trout pout."

Tastes like . . . victory.

I haven't seen anyone handle an axe like this since Kurt Russell in *Backdraft.*

Donkey Kong on the Guinness factory tour.

**Forties and dice doesn't mean
Bud and Dungeons & Dragons.**

"Yo, son, I'm really happy for you, and I'ma let you finish, but I think this is the best mustache of all time."

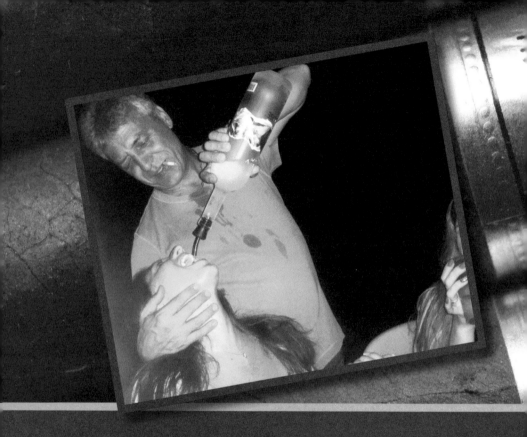

A new twist on midnight bottle-feeding.

Come for the hair but stay for
the dickie.

A wise man once said, "A woman
is an occasional pleasure, but a
cigar is always a smoke."

"Piggyback fight!"

"I think I just drank kerosene."

Waves get bigger during a full moon.

A hook stuck in his thumb, Dad
bites the silver bullet.

**After a long day at the office,
Dad puts his feet up.**

Now, that's one hog you can ride
without shame.

Dad's handicap is gin.

Thirty years later, those haircuts are back in style.

Superglue mishap or awesome celeBrotion?

"I take it Mom's out of town?"

"Dry wedding, my ass."

"This one gang kept wanting me
to join because I'm pretty good
with a bow staff."

"Hi, I'm Murray!"

Dad's 'stache is a rainbow of
awesome.

Hell and his two angels.

Dad sees four disasters and
starts prioritizing.

Flicking ash and stacking cash.

"I ain't dead yet!"

This dad needs two things: beer pong lessons and an interior designer.

What is love?

"Now pledge allegiance to your mother."

Dad cuts more glass than
Pamela Anderson.

"How am I going to explain this
to your mother?"

Drinking bottles in the nursery.

**The fastest route to happiness:
lowered expectations.**

"Now, this is why I took up fishing!"

"Don't make me chase you, ladies."

King of the Brocean.

Good to see the Iron Sheik is still
alive after all these years.

**Apparently the no-leaning rule
wasn't in place when Dad was in
college.**

Lost love child of Bob Ross?

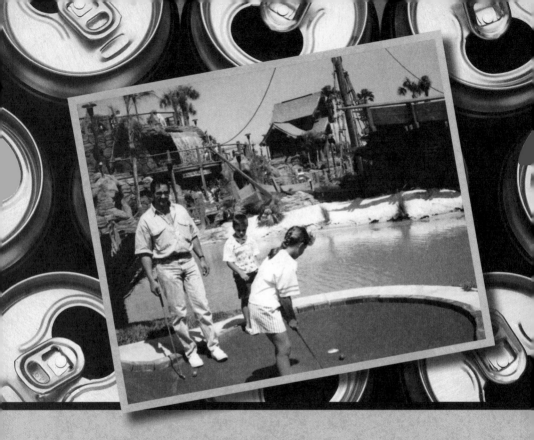

"Sink this putt, sweetie. I want
to see your brother cry again."

Dad's dancing comes with a complimentary "O" face.

"This wasn't what we expected when Dad said he was going to dress up as a wasp for Halloween."

A father, his daughter, and a
young Don Johnson.

Dare we say "Bro'ing the lawn"?

Dad back in the day, late for one
of Jay Gatsby's parties.

No matter the generation, a Bro is a Bro is a Bro . . .

"Size matters not. Judge me by
my size, do you?"

This one's going out to the ladies.

The art of the deal: "Okay, son. I'll give you $10 a week, and in return you will mow the lawn, wash the cars, take out the trash . . ."

"What? She told me to put the
box on my head."

"Move over, Tony Manero, there's
a new king of disco."

Acknowledgments

We want to thank all the BroBible readers who had the audacity to send us photos of their fathers. Your courage, and kind gesture, to memorialize your father—even if he is blackout drunk in the photo—should be applauded. Without you, this book would not be possible.

Thank you to the fantastic folks at Simon & Schuster and Gallery—especially our editor, Jeremie Ruby-Strauss—for giving a group of misfits a chance to pay homage to the greatest man in every Bro's life. We owe you a beer. Or ten.

Thanks to our families for all your love, support, and patience through every phase of our lives. We know we haven't always made it easy, but somehow you've mustered the strength to stand by us the entire way.

And, of course, we want to thank our own fathers, who not only shaped our lives and our minds, but inspired us to write the captions in this book the only way we knew how: Drunk off our asses.

Finally, to Stephon: For understanding the vision from the beginning, all my love and gratitude. Thank you for your support, wisdom, and unwavering conviction. S + H, DB

Credits

Text by Jason Cammerota and Brandon Wenerd

PAGE ii: Tucker Smith, Matthew Mah, Susan Brown-Kilmer

PAGE vi: Dylan Loch

PAGE 4: George Hadjiyerou

PAGE 16: Brendan Helberg

PAGE 17: Dylan Doyle

PAGE 18: Jeff White

PAGE 19: Ryan Warnberg

PAGE 20: Will Baribault

PAGE 21: Benjamin Pruzan

PAGE 22: Paul Van Wert IV

PAGE 23: Anonymous Bro

PAGE 24: Richard Ryan

PAGE 25: Joshua Deems

PAGE 26: Meg Morrissey

PAGE 27: Conor Kerwin

PAGE 28: Anonymous Bro

PAGE 29: Jessica Beattie

PAGE 30: Chris Martino

PAGE 31: Harrison Hanson

PAGE 32: Caitlin Bahm

PAGE 33: Matt Walker

PAGE 34: Sarah Lang Palenik

PAGE 35: Elias Ronstadt

PAGE 36: Karl Grabbi

PAGE 37: Austin Evans